The Seven S's of Develor

Also in this series

Also by Sue Cowley

The Seven S's of Developing Young Writers

SUE COWLEY

Sue Cowley Books Ltd

2015

Sue Cowley Books Ltd
PO Box 1172
Bristol BS39 4ZJ

www.suecowley.co.uk

© Sue Cowley Books Ltd

First published 2015

Part of the 'Alphabet Sevens' Series

Also in this series:

The Seven C's of Positive Behaviour Management
The Seven E's of Reading for Pleasure
The Seven M's of Writing for a Living
The Seven P's of Brilliant Voice Usage
The Seven R's of Great Group Work
The Seven T's of Practical Differentiation

ISBN: 978-1508715733

Contents

Introduction

In this short guide you will find a host of ideas, strategies and techniques for helping your students to develop their writing, so that they become confident and fluent writers. This book is written from the perspective of both a teacher and an author: it is about helping students become effective writers, and also about showing them why they might *want* to write. This is not just a book about teaching young people to do well in written exams; it is a book about how to develop the next generation of writers.

It is hugely important for young people to be able to write, and preferably to be able to write fluently and expressively, because this will help them achieve success at school, in adult life, and in the workplace. As well as this, though, it is incredibly liberating to be able to express your thoughts, opinions and feelings through the written word. Your students might have the most brilliant ideas in the world, but if they can't write them down, then they cannot record them and other people cannot access them.

As educators, we need to think carefully about the messages we send around writing. Although accuracy and technique are vital, a heavy-handed focus on these areas can de-motivate young writers. At all times, the writing we ask them to do should be about expression and communication – about saying something for a specific purpose, to a particular audience. I often hear of students who are poorly motivated about writing – teachers tell me that some young people don't seem to *want* to express themselves through the written word. With a large percentage of the school day spent on writing, it is crucial that we find ways to make writing feel like a valuable and purposeful activity, rather than just something that our students *have* to do.

This mini guide covers all aspects of learning to become a writer, in a concise but thorough way. It will be useful to primary teachers, and also to secondary English teachers and teachers working in other subject areas where writing is used frequently. You can find tips here on building the physical skills needed for writing, on teaching writing techniques, and on inspiring your students to want to write. You will learn how to assess your students' work for maximum impact, and see how to encourage your young writers to scrutinise and edit their own writing, until it is the best that it can possibly be. I hope you find lots of useful, practical ideas in this book, and also that you find it a source of inspiration, as you go about the vital task of developing young writers.

Sue Cowley
www.suecowley.co.uk

The First S:

Speaking

The First S: Speaking

Writing is an act of communication. Writers share their thoughts and ideas, as they might say them, tidied up and transcribed onto a page. When we write, we edit and adapt our thoughts, and we typically use longer and more complex vocabulary than in speech. But, essentially, the words you are reading now are me talking to you. What all this means is that we can only write what we can say. What this also means is that we can only write *how* we can say as well. We cannot use vocabulary, or phrasing, or constructions in our writing unless we can use them in our speech as well. If your young writers struggle to express themselves verbally, they will struggle to express themselves coherently in writing as well. Conversely, if you get your young writers speaking their thoughts and ideas with confidence, you will help them learn to write with confidence as well.

Teacher Talk

Every time you talk in your classroom, you model speech for your students, and so it is crucial to model talk in the best way you can. This sounds obvious, but it is harder to speak clearly and effectively than you might think, particularly with all the stresses and strains of the typical classroom situation. If you are new to teaching, this is one of the key skills you will develop over your first few years in the job. As you gain in experience, articulate patterns of speech will become second nature. Here are some tips for great teacher talk:

✓ Speak mostly in Standard English: this is particularly crucial for those students who rarely hear it modelled outside school.

✓ Intersperse 'proper' speech with the odd colloquialism, turn of phrase, or slang term. This shows you are human and also helps your students understand that they can play around with language, as appropriate to the context and audience.

✓ Speak mostly in full sentences, adapting the sentence length according to the age and learning needs of your students.

✓ When you use repetition, as often happens in the classroom, adapt the words you use slightly each time. Expose your students to more complex vocabulary through talk, while still retaining the sense of what you are saying.

✓ Avoid punctuating your speech with lots of 'ums' and 'ahs' – speak as fluently as you can. I find it helps to think ahead about my next sentence, as I say the current one.

✓ When giving instructions, use a series of time connectives to highlight the order of what is to be done: 'first … then …. after … finally.' Put a stress on these words, to help your students understand that you are using them to show order.

✓ Use emphasis, pace and tone to give richness and texture to your speech and to help your students pick out meaning. Put a stress on key terms and pause briefly after you say them, to let students assimilate the meaning. Add a questioning tone to your voice when asking questions and a curious tone to increase engagement.

✓ Use self talk and parallel talk, to help your young writers expand their vocabulary, and their knowledge of language constructions. Self talk is the art of speaking your thoughts out loud, for instance saying "I was wondering whether this might work …". Parallel talk means talking through what your students are doing, as they do it. This is especially helpful when working one to one with second language learners. So, you might say, "I can see that you are drawing a house … ah, now it looks like you are going to put a chimney on the roof."

✓ For students who join you with very little English, offer a bank of 'emergency words' – hello, goodbye, toilet, yes, no, drink, eat. Focus on using lots of vocal tone, non verbal gestures and visual prompts, to support EAL learners.

Using Q&A

Every time you use questions, and get answers from your students, you have a chance to help them develop their speaking/thinking, and learn how to express their ideas more clearly. Encourage your students to answer questions using Standard English, and correct grammar. When students use slang, colloquialisms, or abbreviations in their answers, repeat back what they have said using correct English, and encourage them to develop their own speaking. For instance:

Teacher: What should Charlie have done when Alex bullied him?

Student: I would of nutted him, Miss.

Teacher: Could you explain that a bit further for me? Do you mean you would have hit him?

Open questions help your students develop their language skills much more effectively than closed questions. Encourage your students to articulate their ideas, thoughts and feelings by asking 'What do you think...?' type questions, rather than 'What is the answer?' type ones. Give your students lots of chances to ask questions of each other, as well as of you.

Speaking in Context

When we write, we adapt what we say according to the context in which it will be read. We consider the audience who will read our words, and then we adapt the form, structure, style and vocabulary to suit. Use role play and scenarios to put your young writers into different contexts, and to encourage them to think about suiting their talk (and writing) to a specific situation.

✓ Ask your students to imagine themselves as different characters, and talk about how they have to change the way that they speak. For instance, get them to play a politician making a speech in Parliament, a doctor talking to a patient in a hospital, or a cashier dealing with a complaint in a shop.

✓ Have a role play area for young writers, so they can immerse themselves in 'real life' situations. In an infant classroom, your role play area might become a shop, a post office, a home, a Super Hero Base, a vet's surgery, and so on.

✓ A great way to extend children's role play is to write snippets of dialogue on pieces of paper, and to ask the children to incorporate these snippets into their scenario. Your dialogue can guide the action or add dramatic tension: 'Someone help me!' or 'What on earth is that?'

✓ With older students incorporate role play into lessons, for instance asking someone to play a character from a novel, to hot seat them. As students answer questions in role, they should try to mirror the speech patterns used by the character in the book.

✓ Give your students reasons to talk in different contexts during the school day, and at home. For instance, they might take an excellent piece of writing to talk about with the head teacher, or they might do a presentation to the class, or in assembly. They could interview grandparents at home, for a project. Invite parents or other visitors in as well, to give your students a real life audience and context for their speaking.

Speaking as a Character

When they write stories, your students need to consider how different characters speak. This is harder than it sounds – even seasoned novelists find it hard to write convincing dialogue. Dig down into what different characters might do/think/feel, and how they might express that, by using drama activities with your students.

✓ **Capture snippets:** Ask your young writers to capture and bring in snippets of dialogue heard outside the classroom. They might note down an interesting sentence they heard on the bus, or something funny that dad said at home. Share these, and incorporate your favourites into a piece of writing.

✓ **Conscience alley:** (Also known as 'thought tunnel'.) Get your students to create two parallel lines, a person's width apart (this is your 'alley'). Choose a character from a story you have been reading. Now ask for a volunteer to play the character from the story, and to walk down the alley with their eyes shut. As they pass, the children on either side say or whisper a word or sound to them, related to how the character is feeling in a certain situation, or how other characters relate to them in the book. Afterwards, talk about how it felt to be that person.

Talking Stories

Stories are an ancient part of human nature. Long before the written word, oral story telling played a pivotal role for us, because it was a way to pass on our history and knowledge to the next generation. A great way to help your children become confident speakers/writers is to get them to read, memorise and retell stories. Try these activities:

✓ After reading or working on a familiar fairy tale in class, ask your students to re-tell the story to a partner, in their own words.

✓ Share some stories around a camp fire, for instance if you run forest school sessions, or when you take your children on a school camp.

✓ Set a homework in which you ask your children to retell a story from school at home, to their parents.

✓ Explore the stories that are told in different cultures, and in different languages. Ask parents and visitors to come in and share stories from other parts of the world.

✓ Look at Pie Corbett's Story Making and Talk for Writing techniques, around retelling stories, using movements to help the children remember the sequences.

✓ Get your students to do a whole class performance of a story they have memorised, including actions, to an invited audience of parents and carers.

The Second S:

Stimulus

The Second S: Stimulus

Some young people develop a 'do I have to?' attitude to writing. They are not well motivated to write and do not really enjoy it. It is (usually) possible to force young people to write at least something, by threatening a consequence if they refuse. However, this reinforces the attitude that writing is not fun, and your students are unlikely to write their finest prose when under threat of punishment. It is far better to encourage them to *want* to write, by using imaginative, interesting and engaging stimuli. That way, they should hopefully also see writing as something that they choose to do, outside of school, as well as inside.

Warm-ups as a Stimulus

Just as we do a physical warm-up at the start of an exercise class, so it is useful to do a mental warm-up at the start of a period of writing as well. Some of the warm-ups below help clear the mental clutter out of your students' heads so they are ready to write; others will get their ideas flowing. Join in with your students while they are doing these activities, to model the 'teacher as writer'.

Stream of Consciousness: When you say 'go', your students must write for two minutes without stopping. It's important not to stop writing – if they get stuck they should write the same word over and over until they get unstuck. Your students do not have to write *about* anything specific, they should just dump the contents of their brains onto the page. Tell them not to edit their thoughts as they write, just to pour them all out in their writing. Explain to the students that, at the end of the time, they will be free to throw away what they have written if they wish, without anyone ever reading it.

Explain that, in this activity, there is no need for accurate spelling, punctuation and grammar. The students do not need to write in sentences, and no one is going to check their writing over at the end or ask them to correct it. I highly recommend that you join in with your writers – it offers them a great role model and you may also find it incredibly cathartic, especially if you are feeling stressed.

When you are finished, ask your students for some feedback on how it felt to do the stream of consciousness. People often report that it feels very freeing to dump out their thoughts in this way.

Word tennis:

Choose a theme, e.g. chocolate, the sea, fruit, holidays, blue, pets, The Simpsons. The teacher can choose the theme, or the students can nominate one of their own choice. The students should work in pairs, playing tennis with words that occur to them on this theme. To play, the first person throws a word at their partner, who throws one back, and so on until someone pauses or stumbles. The person who pauses loses the point. Play 'best of three' then change to a new theme.

Who Am I?:

Cut out lots of pictures of different people from magazines – include people of different ages, cultural backgrounds, ethnicities, etc. You can do this activity individually, in pairs, or in a larger group. Give each student a picture then ask them to write a short character study of the person, including name, age, personality, hobbies, etc. This could be written as a Top Trumps style card. Talk about what your young writers have written. Challenge them about whether they stereotyped their characters by how they looked. Explain how it is far more interesting and authentic to write against the stereotype.

Pick 'n' Mix:

Fill up a jar with words on folded slips of paper – choose random words, including nouns, verbs, adjectives, etc. Get a volunteer to pull out three words. Working in pairs, your students have sixty seconds to come up with a sentence that includes all three words.

Pass the Story:

This is a classic activity that many of us did when we were children. Ask your students to write the first sentence from a story at the top of a piece of paper, then to pass this to the person on their right. The next person adds a second sentence on the line below the first one, inspired by the story starter, then folds the paper down so that only the second sentence is showing. Pass the paper again, and again write another sentence, each time folding down the paper so that only the previous sentence is showing. After about ten passes, return the paper to the person who began the story. Unfold the paper to see how the story turned out.

Alphabetti Spaghetti:

Choose a letter of the alphabet (it's best not to go for X or Z). Ask your students to each write a sentence in which every word starts with this letter. They should not worry if it does not make sense. For instance: 'An amazing ant always admitted any advantages.' or 'Timmy the Terrible took time to terrorise the totally tentative tribe.'

Objects as a Stimulus

There is something weirdly powerful about having a physical object to inspire writing: a *thing* to which the writer reacts. The object might belong to a character in a story your students go on to write; it might inspire a non fiction writing response. You can also use objects to stimulate writing in all curriculum subjects – a souvenir or leaflet brought back from holiday, for instance, to start off a geography session. It works really well if you and your students come across the object 'unexpectedly' – it just happens to be there in the classroom when you arrive. Who on earth could have left *this* behind?

✓ **Left luggage:** You and your young writers discover a bag left in the classroom. This could be a handbag, with weird or interesting items inside. It could be a suitcase, filled with something specific to a location, weird or unusual. (I once heard about a writing lesson that began with the children finding a suitcase stuffed full of bananas). Write about the kind of character who owns the bag, and what he or she was doing in your room.

✓ **Inspired by nature:** A selection of shells can inspire your students to write about distant lands – describing a desert island, or a strange underwater world. 'Found' objects such as a bird's nests or a skeleton leaf can spark off writing about nature.

✓ **Blast from the past:** Bring in a mobile phone from twenty years ago, an old school book/report, or a ration book from a parent or grandparent who lived through the war. Use these objects from the past to inspire your students to write about what it was like to live ten, twenty, fifty years ago.

✓ **Literary Lego:** Give your students a bag of Lego to work with, including mini figures. Get them to create an image showing the start of a story, or to make a full storyboard using a series of models in different scenes. Alternatively, the students could make a Lego model to summarise a book they have already read, guessing which story the others have chosen.

✓ **Bag/box of story:** Create a series of different bags or boxes, with interesting items inside, to inspire your students to write stories. One bag might contain a pine cone, a bird's feather and some walnuts, while another could contain a memory stick, a photo of an old house and an apple. You can also create themed bags, for instance bags with objects related to the seaside, or nature, or war, or Harry Potter.

Images as a Stimulus

A photo, painting or film has the power to take us 'somewhere else', without us needing to go anywhere at all (just like books do). Use images to stimulate writing – not just about what can be seen directly, but about what is inferred as well.

✓ Show your students a photograph of a landscape, and ask them to look at it carefully. Now get them to close their eyes and imagine themselves stepping into the photo. What can they hear, smell and see? Ask them to turn right, and to walk along. What do they see next?

✓ Find a photo of some animals doing amazing things – on today's news there was a photo of a weasel 'riding' on a bird's back. Get your writers to write 'from the perspective' of the weasel. What is it doing there?

✓ Ask your young writers to bring in their own images to act as a stimulus for writing, for instance 'your favourite family photograph' or 'your favourite holiday snap'. What memories come to mind from this time or place?

✓ Watch a clip from a film. Ask your students to imagine themselves as a character in the film, and to write about the place where they live. Alternatively, turn down the sound and ask your young writers to imagine what the characters are saying, and to create a script for the scene.

✓ Find images of well-known characters and settings from books and films. Take two of these and 'mash them up' together. What would happen if Winnie the Witch landed on the Star Ship Enterprise? What would it be like if Doctor Who met Superman?

Starting with the Senses

The senses are a great stimulus for writing, particularly creative writing. We will often use visual and aural stimuli in classrooms, but typically the senses of touch, taste and smell are rather neglected. To start with the senses:

✓ **See:** Try this 'zoom in' activity. Ask your students to look closely at a scuff or a scratch on their desks, and then to write about it. They might write about what the scuff looks like, how it was made, or perhaps write from the perspective of the desk about when it was scarred.

✓ **Hear:** Music is a great stimulus for writing. Play a piece of classical music to your students, such as Grieg's *In The Hall of the Mountain King* and ask them to write the description of the setting as they listen. Or try a piece of modern music that gives a strong sense of place, such as *Kashmir* by Led Zeppelin.

17

✓ **Touch:** Bring in a variety of objects with specific textures – a patch of mock fur, a teddy bear, a piece of sandpaper, and so on. Ask your students to close their eyes and to focus in on feeling the texture of the object. They could list all the words they associate with that texture, write a series of similes for the texture ('as rough as sandpaper') or use the feeling to trigger a piece of descriptive writing.

✓ **Taste:** Eating can trigger some interesting writing. You could bring some food into class to taste, or ask your students to think about this at lunchtime or at home. Get them to describe the taste of a food in different ways: with a metaphor, using alliteration, in a five word sentence, or as though they are an alien just arrived on Earth.

✓ **Smell:** Scents can trigger long forgotten memories; we often remember smells from way back in our past. Get your students to smell different scents, and to write about what they imagine. Encourage them to 'translate' scents into different senses, for instance what does the smell of mint look like, or what is the sound of a bag of crisps?

You can also remove a sense to inspire writing. For example, get your students to go outside, wearing a blindfold, so that they focus in on the sounds around them. They could work in pairs, with one person making notes as the other describes what he or she hears.

Reading as a Stimulus

Reading acts as a stimulus for writing, and a support for it as well. The more we read, the more words, and combinations of words, we encounter. We hear different writers' voices, and we learn what kinds of writing we enjoy and what kinds we do not. A great piece of advice for any writer is to read as a writer, and write as a reader. When you read, have a dialogue going on in the back of your mind about what works well. If something in a piece of writing makes you smile, or wince, think about what it was which caused that effect. Similarly, when you write, consider how your reader will feel, when you use language in different ways.

For reading to be a useful stimulus for writing, encourage your students to read everything and anything they want (obviously within age appropriate boundaries). Young people will often get really 'into' a single author, and will read a series of books written by him or her, for instance Darren Shan, Jeff Kinney or Malorie Blackman. This is not only a great way to get your students reading a lot, it also helps them get a feel for what we mean when we say that a writer has a 'voice'.

Instead of being particular about what children read, it is best to encourage them to read very widely and with pleasure at the forefront of their minds. Let your students know that, if they are reading a book outside school and they are not enjoying it, it is okay to stop reading it. This can come as quite a surprise to some of them! Give your students access to all different kinds of texts – non fiction as well as stories, pamphlets, brochures, blogs, comics, computer games manuals, magazines, newspapers – the lot.

Samples as a Stimulus

A typical writing lesson often starts with an exemplar text – this gives the students a sense of what you are hoping they will achieve. Samples can give a writer confidence as well, particularly when we take on the 'voice' of another writer, or when we use a similar format or technique. You can also offer samples of vocabulary, and different sentence starters, for your students to use.

✓ Titles make a great stimulus for writing. Try some real book titles, especially ones your students have not read, and ask them what they think these books are about: 1984, The Secret History, Wolf Hall, The Stranger. Make up some of your own titles to inspire writing: The Day the World Went Wrong; My Friend the Alien; The Famous Failure; Whatever You Do Don't Open That Door.

✓ Use a visualiser to display samples of student writing. Ask the students to talk about their own writing when you display it: what words did they choose, why did they choose them, which bits of the writing do they feel work best? It works well to examine samples just after they have been written, while they are 'hot off the page'.

✓ Create a workshop type atmosphere by asking your students to write a short piece, then sharing samples around the class. Encourage your young writers to talk about author intentions – why do they think the person used that specific word or way of phrasing something?

Surfaces as a Stimulus

We tend to think of writing as something that happens with a pen or pencil in an exercise book, or using a keyboard to type on a computer. But it is great fun to let your students experiment with writing on a variety of different surfaces. You might try:

✓ Writing on walls – use large sheets of paper stuck up on the walls, or try 'magic whiteboard' (a removable whiteboard that acts as a temporary surface).

✓ Writing on windows using drywipe marker pens (check with your school first). You can also use white liquid chalk marker pens too, which wash off easily.

✓ Writing on flipcharts, standing up, rather than in books, sitting down.

✓ Adding chalkboard paint to surfaces outside, so your students can write with chalks, or writing directly onto tarmac in the playground.

✓ Designating a 'graffiti wall' outside where students can experiment with graphic logos and designs.

✓ Sticking paper to the underside of desks, so that students can hide to write in secret.

✓ Colouring a piece of paper with different coloured wax crayons, then covering it with black paint and scratching writing into this surface. (The different colours show through which creates a lovely 'rainbow' effect.)

✓ Writing in and on natural surfaces, such as mud and sand, and mark making with materials such as foam or gloop (cornflour mixed with water).

✓ Writing on desks – cover the entire desk with a large sheet of paper or use drywipe markers. This gives a frisson of excitement for the students.

✓ Writing on film/cellophane stuck over the top of a display or on a working wall.

✓ Labelling the classroom environment, for instance writing stories over a map of the world, or adding labels to resources.

Displays as a Stimulus

Display samples of your own, your students', and other writers' work to show what effective writing looks like. If you are going to include negative samples (i.e. what not to do), write your own rather than displaying the work of students. Get your students to annotate and label the 'mistakes' within the writing that is on display. You can also use displays of key words, interesting phrases or fascinating images. A display of samples of a single author's work can help the students see how an author's voice 'runs through' everything he or she writes. For instance, a display of different Michael Morpurgo book covers, with samples of text from each one stuck around them.

Working with Scenarios

A dramatised scenario is a brilliant way to motivate your young writers, and to give them a vivid and powerful sense of purpose and of audience. A scenario is basically a scene that is set up to inspire a response, working from *inside* the story. Your scene can be like a still life, for instance a 'crime scene' that you set up in your classroom. It can also be a living, breathing, evolving event, such as the dragon's egg story below.

Egg on the Roof: I heard this story from a group of teachers, who had spent a week working on the scenario at their school. The children arrived at school on the Monday, to find that a giant egg had 'landed' on the roof of the school. How did it get there? Where did it come from? And, most importantly, what on earth was inside it? The school arranged for a series of visitors to come in, including police officers and fire fighters, to talk about the egg and how they could get it down from the roof.

This scenario led on to the children writing instructions for getting the egg down, stories about dragons hatching out of eggs, and all kinds of other exciting things. I have heard of many similar approaches, for instance an alien object crash-landing in the playground, with the children inspired to write in response to this scenario, or Goldilocks being caught breaking into the classroom to eat the bears' porridge.

IT as a Stimulus

The last twenty years have brought about some amazing developments in the world of technology. The Internet, tablets, smartphones, apps – we have a wide range of options for using technology as a stimulus (or support) for writing. Make sure that you:

✓ Offer tablets, iPads or laptops so that students can record their ideas: this is especially useful for those who struggle to write fluently.

✓ Look at different word processors for your students, with a focus on assistive technology where needed. The Writer app, iReadWrite and WriteOnline are all recommended for predictive text, speech to text and colour setting options.

✓ Explore the range of writing apps that are available for your different devices. Alan Peat has created great apps for teaching writing (www.alanpeat.com/apps.html).

✓ Consider how you might 'flip' your lessons, for instance by asking students to watch a YouTube video at home that relates to the next lesson.

✓ Think about teaching your students to touch type. Although voice recognition software has come on a great deal in recently years, they will spend an awful lot of time typing over their school careers.

The Third S:

Sense of ...

The Third S: Sense of ...

Writing is an act of communication – words written by a writer on a page only come to life when a reader reads them. Every piece of writing is done (or at least should be done) with a strong sense of purpose and a clear sense of audience in mind. We need to help our young writers understand that there is a good reason for them to write, and that a specific audience will, or could, read what they have written. When we talk with young people about why they must learn to write, we need a better answer than 'to pass exams'. By creating a strong sense of purpose for our young writers, we should help them feel motivated to write.

Sometimes a piece of writing has a very specific purpose: to persuade the reader to agree with an argument, or to complain so that something is done. At other times a writer's purpose is more general – a story can entertain, excite, or amuse. Sometimes we might write a private piece that no one else will see – a diary or a poem, perhaps. In these cases, the purpose is a type of cathartic self-expression, with the audience limited simply to oneself. When we teach writing, our students are often given more than one audience for whom to write. The teacher acts as one audience, but there are usually one or more external (often imaginary) audiences as well.

Sense of Purpose

When you plan a writing activity, think about the reasons *why* the students are writing this particular piece. The purpose doesn't have to be world changing – writing can cheer us up as well as being used to campaign for social justice. Talk with your students about the purpose of the writing, before you begin. The stronger the sense of purpose we have as writers, the more we invest in what we are writing. Although the teacher can create imaginary purposes for writing, in a lot of ways it is better to make the purpose feel as genuine and as real life as possible. This shows your young writers what writing can achieve for them. Here are some ideas:

✓ Write a letter to persuade your head teacher to increase the length of playtime;
✓ Write an anti-bullying song, to play to the rest of the school in an assembly;
✓ Write a letter to an aunt, uncle or grandparent, to say how much you love them;
✓ Write a storybook for your younger brother or sister, or for the children in a Reception class;
✓ Write a letter to your MP, to ask for action on a local issue;
✓ Write an email to the local paper, asking them to report on something great that has happened in your school;
✓ Write a blog for young people, explaining the United Nations Convention on the Rights of the Child, and how it impacts on their lives.

Sense of Audience

Ideally, a writer wants a real audience for his or her writing. However, remember that not every piece of writing has to end up being published to an audience. (For every piece that ends up as a finished book, blog or article, I throw away at least ten or twenty ideas and scruffy drafts.) Your students are learning to write, and at the moment their main audience is the teacher. Even so, the more authentic the audience feels, and the bigger that audience is likely to be, the more motivated your students should feel to write. The idea that lots of people are reading and hopefully enjoying what you write is a very powerful motivation to write more. When considering audiences for your young writers:

✓ Consider how important the intended audience is to them, as this will impact on their motivation. For instance, they should hopefully put maximum effort in when they are writing for the head teacher or for a parent, e.g. a Mother's Day poem.

✓ Think about the potential size of the audience – a poem that is published in a school magazine will reach more readers than one displayed on the wall of a classroom. A poem published in a national magazine will reach yet more again.

✓ Some kinds of writing are done to elicit a response in the reader – for instance, a letter might be answered. Where possible, choose audiences that are likely to answer your students' letters. Many authors respond to letters they receive from their fans, so try getting your students to write letters to an author they love. Alternatively, set them up with penpals from a school abroad.

✓ Teachers are, of course, a real audience for their students' work. However, having the same audience all the time tends to stunt your ambition a bit. Consider other adults within and beyond your school as a potential audience, including non-teaching staff, family, local dignitaries, and so on.

Real Audiences

There are lots of ways to give your young writers a taste of how it feels to have their writing published, and to have a real live audience for their work. You might:

✓ Get your young writers to create 'mini books' on different topics, for instance when you are doing a topic on a country or an historical period. These could be put in the school library for others to read, or used as a research base for other classes when they study the same topic.

✓ Publish your students' writing in displays, in your own classroom and around the school. Update writing displays regularly, and encourage students to read them.

✓ Create a school magazine or newspaper, working with a team of student volunteers in a lunch or after school club.

✓ Set up a class blog – recommended sites for doing this include Typepad, Wordpress and Weebly (all free).

✓ Hold a competition across your school, for instance for poetry. Create a pamphlet of entries, with winners in different age categories. This can be sold, with the money raised used to pay for book tokens for the winners.

✓ Encourage your students to enter online competitions and challenges. You could try the 100 word challenge, where young writers write 100 words and get feedback (www.100wc.net). Try Lend me Your Literacy too – a site where young writers around the world can share their writing (www.lendmeyourliteracy.com).

✓ If you want to put the boat out, it is relatively simple these days to self publish your students' writing online in ebook format, and also in a paperback. Two good places to start exploring this option are Kindle direct publishing (KDP) and Createspace.

Finding your Form

Where the writer has a clear sense of purpose and of audience, the writing often chooses its form for itself – it is blatantly obvious which form is best to use. If I am writing to complain about a faulty product, I am unlikely to write a poem. (Although interestingly there was a news story recently where two university students wrote a Shakespearean sonnet of complaint to a supermarket, and received a poem in return.) It is interesting that as teachers we often start by deciding what form we want our students to write in, rather than letting the purpose of the writing help them pick the appropriate form for themselves. Perhaps sometimes we should think about working the other way around.

When exploring form:

✓ Talk about the purpose of different forms; a single form often has several possible uses. A poem might make us laugh, cry or create a visual picture for us. A letter could be used to complain, persuade or share news.

✓ Consider how you can subvert the 'traditional' form for a piece, as this makes for an interesting writing experience. Sometimes it works well to make a serious point using satire or humour, rather than writing a traditional essay or polemic.

✓ Choose a character first then write in role as that person in order to find the best point of view. For instance, if you were writing in role as the Wolf, what would be the best form to tell the Three Little Pigs that they do not *really* need to be scared of you?

The Fourth S:

Skills

The Fourth S: Skills

Writing is a highly skilled activity. We must make the right marks on a page so our readers can tell exactly what we want to say. Every young writer needs to develop a set of physical skills in order to write: coordination, dexterity, strength, posture and stamina. My book *The Road to Writing* (Bloomsbury, 2013) takes a detailed look at how you can develop these mark making skills in early years settings. Young writers must also acquire a specific set of technical skills: an understanding of the link between spoken words and written ones; the spelling, punctuation and grammar techniques currently referred to as 'SPaG'.

Coordination

Young writers need to develop eye to hand and eye to finger coordination, to be able to shape letters, and then to write words. They must learn to coordinate the two sides of their bodies, so the left hand holds the page still, while the right hand forms the words, or vice versa if they are left handed. Children build up their coordination over time, and some children find it much harder to develop than others. At first, babies build coordination from the bottom upwards, and from the shoulder out. In other words, their heads are wobbly to begin with and they can't do much with their fingers when they are small. Encourage your children to move in every way that you can – both large movements and small ones are useful for the emerging writer. Any fun, physical activity helps build coordination. For instance:

✓ **Art and craft:** drawing, colouring in, painting, tearing, cutting, sticking, wrapping, threading, weaving.

✓ **Physical education and dance:** balance beams, throwing and catching, climbing, cycling, skipping, hopping, creating shapes with their bodies.

✓ **Music:** using drum sticks, hitting notes on a keyboard, banging cymbals, ringing bells.

✓ **Drama:** manipulating props and invisible objects, playing with puppets.

✓ **Our World:** water play, sand play, small world play, digging, planting, cooking, using chopsticks, using tweezers, tying knots.

Include lots of activities where students move one side of the body independently from the other (this is known as bi-lateral integration). Activities using a bat and ball, and many dance steps, help develop these bi-lateral movements.

Dexterity and Handwriting

It takes plenty of practice for your young writers to develop their dexterity. At first, their marks will be wobbly and may not look much like letters. But with time they become more adept at making the shapes. To develop the dexterity needed for handwriting, there is no substitute for practice, because they need to place these movements firmly into their physical memories. Repetition is the only way to do this. Here are some tips for early handwriting:

✓ Remember that any kind of mark made with a writing tool is a form of 'handwriting'. The more chances and inspirations there are to make marks, the more dexterous your children will become.

✓ When you introduce a new letter, get your children to form it in the air, using an imaginary pencil. Encourage them to make the correct movement with their whole arm, several times over, to embed it into their physical memory.

✓ Get children to write new letters in sand, or shaving foam, or using other textured resources, as well as on paper.

✓ When 'proper' handwriting begins, have a very clear focus on correct letter formation. It is essential to get good physical skills in place early on, as it is much harder to break a bad habit once it is formed.

✓ Show your children how to use the correct pencil grip and keep an eye out for those who are having problems. Where pencil grip is poor, consider whether you need to spend more time getting these children to build hand and finger strength, rather than pushing on regardless.

✓ Get your children to use a pencil to trace over dotted line letter shapes on the page, before attempting to form letters freehand. Ask them to focus carefully on forming the shapes correctly. When older students experience problems with letter formation, take them back to this stage so they get the correct movement into their physical memories.

✓ With young students, set aside a time for daily handwriting practice, for instance ten minutes each morning. Encourage the children to do this practice automatically, independently, and quietly.

✓ Fit handwriting practice into any spare five minutes: laminate some handwriting worksheets so your children can practise them over and over again. Send some of these sheets home, for homework practice.

✓ Don't ask young students to write for very long periods of time, without taking a break. If you see children scrunching their hands to get rid of a cramp, stop and get everyone to have a quick shake out.

- ✓ Have a specific book for handwriting practice, with sets of two lines, so students can practice forming small letters (a, c) and tall letters (l, k). For those who find it hard to form small letters, it can help to use paper where the bottom half of the line is highlighted.
- ✓ Find out which children in your class are left handed, and be aware that they need to form their letters in a slightly different way. You can find letter formation charts online, for children who are left handed.
- ✓ Be conscious that it is often harder for children who are left handed to write, because they cover the letters with their hands as they write. They also have to push rather than pull the pen across the paper.
- ✓ Some children struggle with putting finger spaces between words. For these writers offer a smiley sticker to go between each word when they get the space big enough. Alternatively, give the child a plastic finger to use as a finger spacer for writing.

Ideally, letter and word formation should become subconscious for young writers, leaving as much mental space as possible for ideas to flow freely. It can help to think of handwriting as a dance that fingers do on the page. To write (or dance) well, you need to be supple, know the movements, and be able to do them without thinking. If you are focused on forming the movements, it is hard to express yourself creatively.

Handwriting and Older Students

After a period of neat handwriting, this skill can sometimes go downhill as students get older, especially after the transition to secondary school. Here are some thoughts on dealing with handwriting problems that can occur later on:

- ✓ Have high expectations of the handwriting your students can achieve. Where possible, look at samples of writing from earlier on in their school careers – ask your primary feeder schools to send you these. Show these to individual students, so they know that you know what they are capable of doing.
- ✓ If handwriting is very poor, consider why. Does the student have poorly developed fine motor control, is it about pen grip, or is it to do with motivation?
- ✓ Consider the most appropriate strategies in the light of what you discover. If fine motor control is an issue, offer activities for the student to build strength. Make these seem more fun, by introducing them as an 'exercise programme', for the whole class.
- ✓ Sometimes a student will sacrifice neatness for speed – take care that you don't put young writers under pressure to write fast, if their handwriting becomes illegible.
- ✓ Let your young writers experiment with different writing implements, for instance trying out an ink pen, a soft pencil or a black felt tip, rather than a biro.

Don't mistake neatness for great thinking or interesting ideas. It's easy to mix up the two, and subconsciously to think that a neat piece is better written.

Strength

Young writers must build up their finger strength to write, especially when doing so for long periods. Strength usually develops as a child grows, although some children with special needs or disabilities may not develop their strength so quickly. Happily, all of the activities that develop coordination develop finger and hand strength as well. Once your young writers have built their strength, they must work on it to sustain it. This needs regular practice, so it is a good idea to:

✓ Have set periods of time devoted to the act of sitting down and writing. Spice these up by thinking about creative stimuli – incorporate multi sensory elements to make it feel engaging.

✓ Have a clear expectation of how your young writers behave during writing time. I recommend that you ask students to write in silence, unless they are doing pair or group activities.

✓ Give children lots and lots of reasons to write, for short and long periods: scribbling notes and writing on whiteboards, as well as doing longer pieces.

✓ Find creative ways to stop your young writers from distracting themselves, and each other. A fun idea is to give each child a poker chip. If they want to ask a question, they must cash in their chip. This encourages them to think carefully about whether their question is worth asking.

✓ Allocate plenty of time for children to build their finger and hand strength in other ways: doing arts, crafts, gardening, den building, etc.

Building Finger Strength

To help young writers build strength in their fingers, wrists and hands, incorporate physical exercises into your classroom routine. All these activities build dexterity as well as strength:

✓ Make fists with both hands then stretch out your thumb and return it to the fist. Repeat with each finger, in turn, several times.

✓ Put both hands out flat in front of you. Bring your thumbs in to your palm, then back up. Move along the fingers in turn, repeating several times.

✓ Place your hands on your knees, in a slightly curved position, as though you going to play the piano. Play imaginary notes, up and down your fingers.

As well as exercising their hands and fingers, encourage your students to manipulate a pencil to increase strength and dexterity:

✓ Hold a pencil in a tripod grip. Now walk your fingers up to the other end of the pencil and back down again, maintaining a tripod grip.

✓ Hold a pencil in a normal grip. Now twirl the pencil around and around as though it is a baton.

Pencil Grip

It is really important for young writers to use a pencil grip that is comfortable, and which can be sustained for long periods of time. When your students do external exams, they need to write quickly and neatly under pressure. If they use a poor pencil grip, their fingers or hands may cramp. At first, small children tend to use a 'fist grip' but over time you can help them develop this into a 'tripod grip'. The best way to demonstrate this is to ask your children to make a tripod shape with their thumb, index and middle fingers. The pencil (or pen) then sits in the tripod, with the index finger on top and the shaft of the pencil resting on the webbed part of the hand between the thumb and index finger.

A writer needs to press much harder to make a mark with a biro, than with a pencil or a felt tip. At first, give your children lots of access to writing materials that make a mark easily (charcoal is great, although very messy). It can work best to use a soft pencil, B or 2B rather than HB, as this marks the page more easily.

Posture

Your young writers will spend a lot of time writing over the course of their school careers, so it's vital they learn to sit properly. This will help them with their handwriting, and also allow them to write for longer periods without getting a backache. Encourage your students to sit upright and to keep their shoulders relaxed and level when they write. Check that chairs are at the right height for tables. When writing or typing, your elbows should be roughly level with the desk. You could offer shorter students a cushion or a different chair, to ensure they sit at the right level.

Building Stamina

Stamina is about the strength of your fingers, and also about the strength of your will. At first, children only have the stamina to write for short periods of time, but with the right motivation they should build this up quickly. It is motivation that is key to stamina: whether this is the motivation to get started, or the motivation to keep going. It is hard work on the eyes to stare at a page for long periods of time, so children need to build up this stamina too.

To help your children build stamina, give them valid reasons to write, and interesting audiences to write for. Help them feel inspired, by using interesting and creative approaches: writing is essentially inspired communication, so inspire them to communicate. Gradually increase the length of time you ask your children to write: give them opportunities to write quickly, to scribble notes, as well as times where they are asked to really concentrate and focus. Keeping a private diary can be a great way to build your writing stamina over time.

Technical Skills

The technical skills of reading and writing develop at around the same time, in the first few years of school. However, children gain lots of pre-reading and pre-writing knowledge before this – for instance, an understanding that books contain text, which is made up of squiggly symbols and which contains meaning. Some of the key technical skills for early reading and writing are around an awareness of how sounds in speech relate to sounds in letters and words, and the ability to pick out those sounds in the environment around us.

As young writers develop, we gradually focus more on their spelling, punctuation and grammar. It's useful to consider *why* these are important: what exactly do they do for writers and readers? Firstly, they are about clarity of meaning – they allow us to understand exactly what the writer intends; secondly, they are about letting the reader focus on the ideas, without distraction; and thirdly they are about a certain elegance and style – a 'correctness' in the use of language and tone.

Phonological Awareness

In order to write, children need to 'get' the link between speaking and writing. They must develop their awareness of speech, and of sounds in the world around them. Some children are more adept at this than others – typically these children make rapid progress with reading and writing. If you notice a child who struggles with this, speak to your

SENCo. There can be physical causes at play, for instance glue ear. Here are some ways to help your children develop phonological awareness:

✓ Practise listening and picking out sounds in different situations and contexts – to soundtrack CDs, to birds and nature outside in a garden or forest area, talking with others one to one and in groups.
✓ At first, let children experiment with getting across meaning, without too much of a focus on spelling. When they start out, 'scweak' is fine for 'squeak', 'wons' is fine for 'once'.
✓ Incorporate lots of oral storytelling, music, songs and poetry into your classroom.
✓ Encourage your children to learn how to focus, and listen, paying full attention to what they are hearing. Have periods of quiet concentration during each day.

Spelling

Reading is crucial for spelling: if we see a word spelled correctly a million times, eventually that word becomes fixed in our mind's eye. Knowledge about common letter blends can really help as well – ough, tion, aught. Make sure that you:

✓ Create word banks for your young writers, categorised by subject area, topic, or grapheme. These could go on a wall, with Velcro on the back, or in their books.
✓ Offer your students lists of subject specific spellings to learn. Over time they will build up a sizeable bank of spellings for different subjects.
✓ Get your students to write spelling corrections, several times over, in the back of their writing books.

✓ Set regular spelling tests, to encourage your students to revise spellings, and as a way of checking who needs support.
✓ Give your students plenty of strategies for spelling (see the section below). Talk to them about the techniques people use to retain spellings.
✓ Try not to let students get into bad habits – often they know how to spell the word, for instance their/there but they do not focus enough on getting it right.

Try some backwards spelling as a fun warm up to start lessons: the students close their eyes and spell words backwards in their heads. Start by spelling your full names backwards, then move on to more complex vocabulary. Discuss the different strategies they use in order to get this right.

Strategies for Spelling

One of the best ways to remember spellings is to find a way to link them with something you already know. The link might be visual, aural, via etymology, a mnemonic, and so on.

✓ As younger children learn new words, try this 'write-build-decorate' mini whiteboard idea. Ask the children to divide their whiteboard into three columns: 'write', 'build' and 'decorate'. In the first column the children write out the word, in the second column they build it with magnetic letters, and in the third column they draw and decorate it in bubble writing.
✓ When your students learn phonemes for reading, get them to find banks of words with the same combination

for writing. For instance, a homework to find ten words with the 'ay' sound.

✓ Find the relationships between the spelling/meaning of words students already know, and the spellings of new words. Look for groups of related words, such as one/only/once or kind/kindly/kindred.

✓ When learning longer words, encourage your writers to look out for the words that are *inside* them. For instance, inside the word 'encourage' are 'courage', 'our', 'rage' and 'age'.

✓ Some words stick easily, especially those that are spelt as they sound. With other words the normal pronunciation complicates things. Get your young writers to sound these words in a 'spelling voice' when writing them, saying 'Feb – **RU** – ary' or 'sep – **AR** – ate'.

✓ When you're learning to spell, it is helpful for some learners to look at words as wholes, rather than breaking them up as they do when using phonics. 'Does it look right?' is an important question to ask/answer.

✓ Some tricky letter combinations and words translate into great mnemonics – 'big elephants can always understand small elephants' for because, or 'oh u lucky duck' for the letter combination 'ould'. Get your students to make up their own mnemonics for spellings they find difficult.

✓ Etymology is fascinating and is a great way into spelling. Look at the roots of 'psy' and 'beau' to give your students an insight into how languages steal from each other.

Handling Homophones

Homophones often cause confusion for young writers, especially common ones such as they're, their and there and son/sun. Your students need to see how and why the words are different, and find a link to fix that knowledge into their brains. To help them do this:

✓ Look for logical reasons why words are spelt differently. For instance: 'their' describes something belonging to someone, so it has the letter 'i' in it (I own it); words with 'ere' in them often describe a place ('there', 'here').

✓ Get students to draw doodles of words to represent the thing being described, for instance 'roar' coming out of a lion's mouth, and 'raw' inscribed on a piece of meat.

✓ Have posters on your walls of the most commonly used homophones, so your students can refer to them.

✓ Create fun sentences that include two or three homophones: 'Which witch is the wicked witch?' Add graphics to the sentences and display them on the walls.

✓ Get the students to make posters with homophones on them to display, adding graphics/mnemonics.

✓ Use one of the many apps for practising homophones.

Perfecting Punctuation

Have you found that, despite teaching punctuation techniques repeatedly, some of your young writers still fail to use them properly in their writing? With punctuation, the knowledge of how it should be used needs to be in place, but it is the willingness and determination to get it right, and the understanding of *why* it matters, that is crucial. Many young writers run one sentence into another, or write overly long sentences. The problem is, when they do this they get into the habit of writing streams of unpunctuated prose.

✓ As well as teaching your students how to use punctuation, and what the different marks are for, talk to

44

them about *why* punctuation matters. Punctuation is not about the writer – it is about the reader, and it is about making sense.

✓ When a student presents you with a poorly punctuated piece of writing, read it back to them as it is punctuated, even if this means you do not breathe until the end of the paragraph. Now ask the student to read it back to you and identify where he or she needs to breathe, exclaim, ask a question, and so on.

✓ Encourage your students to use 'mental sentence formation'. Ask them to compose each sentence inside their heads, before they write it down. Insist that they speak the sentence out loud, to you or to a partner, before they put it onto the page. Is it actually a single sentence, or would it be better split in two?

✓ Use cut and paste punctuation activities. Take a simple piece of text and use correcting fluid to take out the punctuation marks. As you white out each mark, keep a tally of how many full stops, commas, exclamation marks, etc. there were in the text. Place these at the bottom and then get your young writers to return them to the piece of text, in exactly the right places.

✓ Probably the best way for your students to remember where to put capital letters, is to remember that they are for Special Things: names, proper nouns, the start of a sentence. You could make a display of lots of Special Things to go on your wall.

✓ Many young writers (and adults) catch 'exclamation mark disorder'. The writer feels that the only way to make his or her writing exclaim is to throw in lots of exclamation marks. To solve 'exclamation mark disorder', explain that *writing* can exclaim, and that we do not need to show exclamation with the mark itself.

Perhaps give your students a 'ration' of exclamation marks to use in a piece/day/week.

Writing Speech

There is nothing particularly complicated about using speech marks, so long as your young writers remember that all spoken words and punctuation marks go *inside* the speech marks. Here are some ways to help them understand this:

✓ Teach your young writers the saying: '66 and 99, new speaker, new line'.
✓ Translate speaking that is in a speech bubble, into speaking that uses speech marks. Use extracts from comics to do this activity, as this makes it much more fun. If you are good at art, you could do some comic style drawings for the students to 'translate'.
✓ Make a 'speech mark sandwich'. Explain to your students that the speech marks are the bread, the spoken words are the filling, and the punctuation is the sauce (ketchup, mayonnaise, HP). When we make a sandwich, the sauce always goes on the inside of the bread, and this is where their punctuation goes too.
✓ Do a similar activity, using a washing line. The children peg up their speech marks and punctuation, making sure that the spoken words go inside the marks.

Perfecting Paragraphs

Quite a few young writers struggle with using paragraphs in their writing. I suspect this is because they see writing as something where you start at the beginning and finish at the end. Encourage them to plan ahead to understand the internal structure of a piece, and to explore where different

46

ideas should go. To help your young writers perfect their paragraphs:

- ✓ Ask students to plan longer pieces of writing before they start – block out the content of each paragraph, for instance using a scaffold or framework. Although it's tempting to write in blocks, and then paragraph afterwards using a // symbol, this encourages bad habits that then need to be broken.
- ✓ Help your writers understand why we change to a new paragraph: a change of place, person, speaker, time, idea or focus. Work through some pieces of text with your writers, identifying the reasons why the writer started a new paragraph where they did.
- ✓ Get your young writers to use different coloured pens to write different paragraphs. Ask them to explain *how* and *why* the content is different.

Getting to Grips with Grammar

When we learn to speak our native language, we build a subconscious understanding of its grammatical rules. We know how our mother tongue works, because we have heard it spoken all around us, since the day we were born. When we begin to write, we mimic the grammatical constructions we have heard. Consequently, the more Standard English your students speak, and the more books they have read, the better able they will be to write in grammatically correct English. If a student always hears and says "would of", you may struggle to get him or her to put "would have" when writing. There are also implications for students who have English as an additional language: that plenty of practice in *speaking* English in different contexts is

47

vital, alongside a growing understanding of the internal structures of English. When teaching grammar:

✓ See grammar as something you spot at every opportunity, rather than it being a discrete subject taught in 'grammar lessons'.
✓ Find every opportunity to use basic grammatical terms, so your students become familiar with them. When taking a register, ask your children to answer with their name and an adjective – Smart Sam or Amazing Annie.
✓ Find links between the names of grammatical terms, and what they describe, to help your students remember them. For example, an adverb 'adds to' a verb.
✓ Get your young writers to play around with language, to explore the different effects they can create. For instance, what happens when they replace a passive verb, such as 'threw' with a more forceful, active one like 'hurled' or 'chucked'?
✓ Start with one type of word, for instance a noun, and then work outwards, adding different effects to explore the impact they have. If we start with 'a dog', what happens if we add the colour 'brown', then if we add the word 'barked', and 'loudly'?
✓ Experiment with word order too. What happens if we start a sentence with an adverb, or if we begin a sentence with a verb? How does it change the sound, sense and feel of what we have written when we adapt the order of the words?

The Fifth S:

Structures

The Fifth S: Structures

All good writing has an internal structure that helps it hang together, flow and make sense for the reader. To help young writers develop, we can show them how to pick apart the internal structures of other people's writing, for instance through story-mapping. They can use this analysis of structure to give them a model on which to build their own writing. By offering writing frames and scaffolds, we help our students build up their confidence and learn more about how these internal structures work.

Structures for Thinking about Writing

As well as exploring structures *within* writing, your students can also use writing to help their thinking. Young writers often work in a linear way, but in order to write effectively, they need to see writing as being about building and constructing text, rather than about moving from the start to the finish. Teach your young writers how to use lists, notes, diagrams, plans, brainstorms and mindmaps. Talk about how writers make a series of decisions about form, audience, viewpoint, style and timing. Show them that brainstorming, researching, mapping, selecting, planning, editing, redrafting and proofing are as much a part of 'writing' as the writing process itself.

✓ Don't always make all the decisions about form and audience for your students – let them experiment with different forms and audiences during the planning stages.
✓ Show your students how to use diagrams to plan a piece of writing, for instance by using a series of mini

brainstorms, one for each paragraph of a non fiction piece.

✓ Help them learn how to use colour within planning structures, for instance to identify themes or group ideas together.

✓ Show them how other writers use writing to build their thinking, by sharing first drafts and annotated/edited drafts, for instance of well known stories or poems.

✓ Celebrate structures for thinking about writing, by having plans for writing on your walls, as well as finished end products. Show the 'sequence' of thinking, planning then writing in a 'working wall' type display.

✓ Examine the 'history' of your students' writing, from first ideas to final presentation, by keeping a series of drafts as they write a piece.

✓ Get your young writers to practise going backwards as well, taking a 'finished' piece of writing and summarising it in a shorter form, such as a mindmap or a diagram.

Making the Structures Explicit

As you model writing for your students, articulate the thinking that goes on inside your head. Talk about how you shape the writing as you do it: express your decisions about structure, word choice, expression, and why you make those particular choices. Encourage your students to participate in the decision-making process as well. For instance, saying:

✓ *"I'm going to move this sentence to the next paragraph, because I think it links in better with the ideas there."*

✓ *"I'm trying to think of a better word for this ... can anyone give me any suggestions about what words I could try instead?"*

✓ *"I feel this bit is too wordy, which words can I cut without changing the meaning?"*

By articulating your own thought processes, you help students understand the concept of a 'writing voice'. That all the time writers are working, they are thinking through the expression/ideas in their heads, to try and make the writing work better. It also helps them see that editing is part and parcel of writing – you don't always write first and edit later – both aspects can take place simultaneously.

Exploring Writing Structures

Different types of writing require different structures: a poem has a structure entirely different to that of a letter, a recipe is written in a different way to a report. Within those overall structures, there are other structures as well – for instance, the way that sentences or paragraphs are constructed or ordered. To develop your students' understanding of structures:

✓ Analyse lots of different samples of text – what kind of structures do they use and more importantly *how can we tell?* Use highlighters to identify techniques. Cut apart pieces of text and move them around to explore the effects that different structures have.

✓ Give your students small snippets of text, just a few words or a couple of sentences, to see how much text they need to identify the structure and consequently the form. How could they tell that a single sentence was from a newspaper report, without seeing a headline?

✓ Identify 'typical phrases' are used in different kinds of writing. For instance a recipe will use phrases such as 'You will need …' and 'Preheat the oven to …'.

✓ Go through different pieces of text to identify a series of useful 'sentence starters'. Display these 'sentence starters' on your walls, to give students a reference point.

✓ Experiment with different sentence structures, by giving specific targets for each sentence within a piece of writing. For example, your 1st sentence must have 5 words, your 2nd sentence must start with an adverb, your 3rd sentence must not use the letter 'e', and so on.

✓ Look at the impact of internal structures on how a piece of writing works. Take two pieces of writing – one simple and one complex – and get your students to count the number of words in each sentence. Talk together about the impact of different sentence lengths. Is longer necessarily better?

✓ Ask your students to go through a piece of writing, to highlight how many words there are with more than three syllables, or how many words they do not understand. (You might like to introduce your students to the 'Flesch-Kincaid Readability Test', which measures how difficult a piece of writing is to comprehend.)

✓ When introducing a new form, give your students a framework within which to work. For instance, your 'letter framework' might have a box for the address, the word 'Dear ….' at the start and 'Yours sincerely,' at the end. This is particularly useful for those who struggle with writing, or who lack confidence.

Story-mapping

A great way to help your young writers understand structures within stories is to get them making story 'maps'. This approach has been popularised by Pie Corbett and Julia Strong, through their 'story-making project' and 'talk for writing' methods. The idea is that the students de-construct and then re-construct stories, adding in new elements of their own, to build their confidence and knowledge about writing.

✓ Read through a familiar story with your class (fairytales work well, because your students are likely to be familiar with them). Talk together about the sequence of plot events in the story. What happens first, next, later, finally?

✓ Work together with your students to draw the story out as a diagram. Use images and symbols to show: who, what, where, when and why. Draw the story chronologically, and link the events together with arrows.

✓ Show your students how, by changing a few of the elements in the story, they can use this map to create a story of your own. For instance, instead of three little pigs their story might have three big bears. If they wish, your students can subvert the conventions of the story, for instance the wolf could be allergic to bears, and it might be his sneezing that brings down their houses.

✓ Re-tell stories orally, as a group, using actions to show elements of structure (for instance, holding an index finger up to show 'first' or a palm facing outwards to show 'finally'.). You could use Pie Corbett's actions, or develop some of your own, in conjunction with your children. Present your stories to different audiences, for instance to other classes, or to parents.

Structuring a Writing Book

Think carefully about the way in which you want your students to structure their writing books. Consider how and where you and they will fit in elements such as planning, edits, corrections, spellings, notes, comments, and so on.

There is no one correct way to set out a writing book, but here are some useful suggestions I have picked up over the years:

✓ Include a set of marking symbols at the start of the book to give you and your students an agreed way of making corrections. Talk with your students about what each symbol means. Encourage them to use these symbols when editing.

✓ Ask students to write on the right hand page, leaving space on the left for comments, notes, edits, etc. Or, write on alternate lines, so that there is space underneath each line for notes.

✓ Allow your writers to include notes, diagrams, jottings, etc. in their writing book, as well as blocks of prose. Alternatively, consider whether to give your students a book for scribbling notes and drawing diagrams, and another for writing.

✓ At primary level, consider using one writing book for writing in all curriculum subjects. This makes it easier to share progress with parents, and it also shows that writing is not just something that happens in literacy lessons.

✓ Have a book where students do longer pieces of writing, or where they write on particular topics or interests. They could use this 'Learning Log' at home as well.

Structures for Analytical Writing

When writing analytically, young writers will tend at first to list a series of points, rather than explaining each one in depth. Help your students learn how to write analytically, by teaching them my 'SEED' technique. This technique is useful for any kind of non fiction writing, whether an essay, a brochure, a report, etc. 'SEED' stands for Statement, Evidence, Explain, Develop.

- ✓ **Statement:** Make a point about something you know to be true, something you believe, or a viewpoint that you want to argue.
- ✓ **Evidence:** Give evidence to support your view, for instance in the form of a quote, a fact, or an example.
- ✓ **Explain:** Show the reader how your *evidence* supports your original *statement*.
- ✓ **Develop:** Move laterally, to draw out wider links.

Probably the best way to understand how 'SEED' works is to show you a couple of examples:

Writing about the rights and wrongs of zoos: [**Statement**] Some people think it is wrong to keep animals locked up in small zoo enclosures. [**Evidence**] In their natural habitat, African lions have a territory of around 100 square miles. [**Explain**] Putting a lion in a zoo enclosure means that it has only a tiny fraction of the space it would have in the wild. [**Develop**] However, some people argue that zoos are vital for conservation efforts, and to protect threatened species.

A tourist brochure for Paris: [**Statement**] Every visitor to Paris simply must visit the Eiffel Tower. [**Evidence**] The Tower is perhaps the best-known building in the capital, and from the top of the Tower you get incredible views of the city. [**Explain**] The Eiffel Tower is such a famous icon of Paris that you will want to take lots of photographs from the top, to show your friends when you get home. [**Develop**] The Tower is so popular, it has had over 250 million visitors since it opened – make sure you join them!

The Sixth S:

Scrutiny

The Sixth S: Scrutiny

One key way for young people to develop their writing is for you to scrutinise it and to offer constructive feedback. After this you get your students to respond to the feedback that you (or others) have given, by editing and adapting what they have done. Through this process, your young writers learn to check, and edit, and adapt, and improve, their writing for themselves. Eventually, they can let go of your steadying hand, and race off by themselves as fully fledged writers. Scrutiny is not just about marking, though, it is about understanding what it means to be a writer: that you must take a magnifying glass to your writing and scrub it until all the imperfections are gone.

Although we often think of editing as something that is done when a first draft is complete, in reality a writer edits constantly to fix errors, correct grammar, clarify meaning, ensure flow, adapt vocabulary, and so on. When you assess your students' writing, and give them feedback on how they can approve, you mirror this self-scrutiny process. Aim to share this self-editing process as much as possible, either through talking about editing together, as you do it, or via a written dialogue in your students' books.

Safe, Secure Scrutiny

In order to be in a position to edit your own writing, and to feel comfortable with other people critiquing it, you need a certain level of confidence. It is odd, really, that we expect our youngest writers to be open to criticism of their work, when as adults we find it so hard to accept. Explain to your young writers that scrutinising their writing does not mean that it is rubbish, or that you do not like it. Rather it is just the way that writers work. Scrutiny is not about a teacher doing something to a student, but about a student and teacher working to improve writing together, until the student learns to do this alone. To help your students feel safe and secure when you critique them:

✓ Write texts yourself, for your students to scrutinise. Show yourself as a writer, even (especially) if you don't feel very good at it. Put yourself on the line, just like you ask your children to do.

✓ Bring in some examples of writing you did when you were a child, to show your students that you were not always as proficient as you are now.

✓ Create some fictional characters to leave samples of work on your whiteboard, walls, desk or door for your students to read. One character could have poor spelling; another might forget to punctuate; another could be an expert writer. Look at these samples and talk about how they might be improved, or what is already good about them. How would your students say these things to the characters, if they met them in person?

✓ Help your students feel secure by insisting that they treat the other students in the group with respect. Encourage them to use positive language, even when giving criticism, and crack down on any disrespectful comments or rudeness.

✓ Always balance the positive with the negative, especially for those children who most struggle to write. Use '3 stars and a wish': note 3 good points about a piece of writing, and one wish about what could be improved. Try the acronyms 'www' (what worked well) and 'ebi' (even better if).

✓ When you show a sample to highlight a particular aspect, make a point of checking with the child first that it is okay to share his or her work.

Balanced Scrutiny

As an educator, you need your students to learn how to assess and correct their own writing, and you will also need to assess and correct their writing as well. However, the last thing you want to do is to put them off writing altogether. Even as an author, I still feel vulnerable when I hand my writing over to others to judge (whether to an editor or to my readers). Imagine how it must feel for our students, particularly for those who have weak literacy skills, to have every piece of writing checked, scrutinised, and corrected. Another issue to consider is whether we end up stilting our young writers, and taking away a little of the pleasure in writing, when we insist that they pick at and adapt every single piece of writing they do. To avoid this:

✓ Sometimes, let your students write a piece of writing that *no one will ever look at.* When it is finished, be brave enough to let them screw it up and throw it away. (This works well for the stream of consciousness activity in Section Three.)
✓ Nominate some pieces of writing that you will not assess – sometimes, let your students write for the pure joy of writing.
✓ Do not see writing as always being about pieces that are edited, marked and completed. Writing is as much about capturing scraps, and ideas, and quick word sketches as it is about a finished product.
✓ Have lots of spaces, places and surfaces in your classroom for writing, and encourage your students to

write whenever they feel the urge. Make it clear that writing is a normal, everyday, useful act, not something that is only found in literacy lessons.

✓ Get your students to gather samples of writing from real life, to show why and how writing has value. They could bring in shopping lists, reminder notes, their parents' old school reports, and so on.

✓ Suggest to your students that they might like to keep a private diary at home, in which they write about their feelings, without the need to share what they have written.

✓ Take care not to focus too heavily on 'secretarial' skills. In other words, do not mix up how neat or accurate a piece of writing is, with how good the ideas or expression are.

Effective Scrutiny

When I scrutinise a piece of my writing, there are two different processes taking place. The first is proof reading – I (constantly) check my writing for any errors of spelling, punctuation, grammar or fact. The second is editing – I cut and adapt and move and change and delete and rewrite and do all those other wonderful things that turn you into a 'writer'. To make your scrutiny as effective as possible:

✓ Have a clear expectation that you want students to check over written work before handing it in, at the very least to correct errors of spelling and punctuation.

✓ Ask students to give a short written assessment of a piece of writing at the end of it, before they hand it over to you. You could focus this, for instance asking them to give a grade for how much effort they put in. Respond to this self-assessment with comments of your own.

61

- ✓ Encourage your students to share their writing with their peers, scrutinising it and responding to it. Give them a format in which to do this, to ensure that they give constructive comments as well as criticism.
- ✓ When you mark writing, give a personalised response as well as a technical one. Talk to your students about how specific bits of the writing made you *feel*, as well as what they made you think.
- ✓ Set aside an allocated time for your young writers to read and respond to your marking – if they do not look at it and react to it, it is basically a waste of your time. A popular acronym for this is 'DIRT' – Dedicated Improvement and Reflection Time.
- ✓ Use coloured highlighters to identify the parts that work well and the parts that need improvement. (However, be conscious that this technique is tricky for any students in your class who are colour blind – about 1 in 13.)
- ✓ Where you use colour coded approaches for marking, make sure that you share what these mean with both the students and their parents. Do not assume that parents will know what the pink/green highlighters mean.
- ✓ Set 'next steps' for improvement when marking work, or when talking to children about their writing. It is often best to focus on one key area at a time, rather than asking them to work on lots of different aspects all at once. Construct these 'next steps' together, whenever possible.
- ✓ Consider having 'mini lessons' in which your students focus on target setting for around ten minutes or so. They could look through writing books from a variety of subjects, to decide on what their focus needs to be. Do not always decide on the targets for them – involve them in setting sensible goals.

How to Scrutinise your Writing

Give your students guidance, to help them understand how to scrutinise their work. Offer questions to guide them through the process. Which parts did they find difficult? Which bits did they enjoy doing? What did they do well? How could they improve their writing further? Sometimes, ask your young writers to scrutinise one particular aspect, rather than identifying all the problems. This is particularly important for those who struggle, and whose writing contains a mass of errors. Have a list of 'self scrutiny' questions on your wall, and in your students' books, so they can refer to it. Here are some suggestions:

- ✓ **Technique:** Is my writing completely free of technical errors – spelling mistakes, missing punctuation and poor grammar?
- ✓ **Word choices:** Did I find exactly the right words for what I wanted to say? Is the vocabulary at the right level of difficulty for the intended audience? Are the words interesting? Did I repeat the same words too many times? (Note: remember that repetition can be used deliberately, for effect.)
- ✓ **Pace and flow:** Does my writing flow easily, with sentences that are just the right length? Did I want the writing to feel choppy, for instance to create tension? Did I want it to feel drawn out?
- ✓ **Structure:** Are my ideas in the right order, and in the right places, so that it makes sense? Are my paragraphs of roughly the same length? In a non fiction piece, have I included an introduction and a conclusion, if appropriate?

- ✓ **Ideas:** Have I linked up my ideas together in a coherent way? Am I saying something new and interesting, or repeating old ideas or clichés?
- ✓ **Figurative language:** Have I used any symbolism, metaphor, personification, etc. in my writing? Did it work? (Note: these techniques can and should appear in non fiction pieces, as well as in stories.)
- ✓ **Sound:** Does my writing sound interesting? Have I added alliteration or repetition to create a powerful effect? Can the reader hear my 'writing voice' coming through?
- ✓ **Audience:** Have I written in a way that suits my intended audience? Which bits of my writing talk directly to or engage with the audience?

The Seventh S:

Style

The Seventh S: Style

A piece of writing can be technically correct and well structured, and yet not have a sense of style. Style is what moves your young writers beyond 'doing some writing' and towards 'becoming a writer'. Style is about developing a unique writing 'voice'; it is about learning how to give pace, rhythm and texture to your writing; and it is also about understanding how to make sure your writing appeals to your readers.

Experimentation and Risk

The best way to develop your writing style is to take risks, to experiment and to get it wrong before you (hopefully) go on to get it right. Making mistakes helps your young writers understand *why* a particular word, structure, idea or form did not work. To encourage your young writers to experiment:

- ✓ Get them to do at least some pieces of writing quickly, in a relaxed way, and not for show, assessment or 'best'.
- ✓ Let them throw away some pieces of writing, making a big thing out of scrunching up the bits that did not work.
- ✓ Praise your students when they take risks in their writing, even if they make mistakes. Make it clear that you are happy for them to experiment.
- ✓ Get your young writers to experiment with taking on the voices of other writers, to help them understand what it is that creates that 'voice'. Choose writers with a distinctive style, such as Ernest Hemingway or Jeff Kinney (author of the Wimpy Kid books).

Figurative Language

Figurative language offers a great way to add texture and depth to writing. Techniques such as metaphor, symbolism and personification take the reader beyond a literal interpretation, and into one where there are hidden layers of meaning. However, these devices are tricky to use well, and can be a bit of a minefield for young writers. When you introduce figurative techniques, take care that your students do not over-egg the pudding. Just because they know what a simile is, does not mean they have to use one in every sentence. Remember too these techniques are not only of use in poetry and other creative forms of writing; I regularly use an extended metaphor to frame a non fiction piece.

✓ **Care with clichés:** When you first introduce figurative language, it is normal for your young writers to resort to using clichés they have heard elsewhere. One useful way to stop them doing this is to brainstorm as many clichés as you can to get them out of the way. Talk to them about *why* it is important for a writer to avoid clichés. Some 'banned' similes might include: 'as big as an elephant' and 'as hot as the sun'.

✓ **Sets of metaphors:** To help your young writers get ideas for using metaphor, ask them to brainstorm ideas in sets. For instance, if the set was 'Weather', metaphorical words and phrases could include: 'a cold glance', 'her face clouded over' or 'his voice thundered'. Some useful sets are: 'travel', 'animals', 'food' and 'geography'.

✓ **Familiar to new:** Take some well-known similes and metaphors, and ask your young writers to freshen them up. A good way to do this is to reference topical events or popular media. For instance: 'they fought like cats and dogs' could become 'they fought like election-crazed politicians' or 'they fought like contestants on Celebrity Big Brother'.

✓ **Drawing the abstract:** For some younger writers, it is hard to conceptualise the level of abstraction needed to understand a figurative turn of phrase. It can help to turn the figurative language into a literal image, for instance drawing a literal 'elephant in the room'.

Engaging the Reader

The best writing engages with the reader, not only through its subject matter and ideas, but because the reader is drawn to listen and react to the writer's voice. Teach your young writers a range of techniques to help them engage their readers, talking with them about *how* and *why* these techniques work. They can:

✓ **Ask questions** to create a sense of dialogue with the reader: *'Can you imagine how it feels to lose your job?'*

✓ **Suggest agreement** to try and bring the reader onside: *'I am sure you agree it is time to make a change for the poorest in society.'*

✓ **Make a personal appeal** to flatter the reader and hopefully elicit agreement: *'As an intelligent consumer, you will notice that this product is superior to all others.'*

✓ **Use alliteration** to give texture, rhythm and movement to the writing: *'The best and biggest benefit of this job is the bonus.'*

✓ **Add an imperative** to ask your reader to feel strongly: *'Make sure that you challenge this cruelty wherever you see it.'*

✓ **Use listing in threes** to give a sense of rhythm and drive: *'She was bold. She was brave. And she was brilliant.'*

68

To develop this idea, play a game of: '*What is this sentence trying to do to me?*' Find some sentences where the author tries to engage the reader, and ask your young writers to talk about author intentions. What is he or she trying to do with the sentence, and how is it done?

Dramatic Tension

Dramatic tension makes the reader desperate to know 'what happens next?' To write exciting, stylish stories, your young writers need to understand what dramatic tension is, and how to create it. They will be familiar with a feeling of dramatic tension, from watching films, but they may not have heard it given a specific name. Creating dramatic tension does not necessarily come naturally to young writers – they must be taught how to do it. There are three basic types of conflict: with oneself, with other people, and with the natural world. To help your young writers create a heightened sense of dramatic tension in their stories, get them to write pieces that:

✓ Incorporate a series of escalating problems, at first small, but gradually increasing in intensity. For instance, a couple go on a drive, their car breaks down miles from nowhere, it begins to snow, they trudge to the nearest house and knock at the door, but do not realise that the house is haunted.

✓ Trap the characters in a confined space, for instance a lift that gets stuck between floors, or underground in a cave, after a rockfall.

✓ Describe someone who is running out of time, for instance the countdown to a bomb going off, or the minutes before a plane runs out of fuel.

Explain to your students that they can also add dramatic tension by varying their vocabulary and sentence structure. They can ramp up the tension by using a series of short sentences and by choosing short, single syllable words, over longer ones. This creates a choppy and tense feel to the style of the writing.

Show, don't Tell

When writing fiction, your young writers need to learn how to show, rather than tell. When writers 'tell', they instruct their readers about the characters – their thoughts, feelings and opinions. When writers 'show', they let their readers make up their own minds. A writer will often 'show' to get lots of information across, because it is the easiest way to do that quickly. Perhaps the best way to understand the difference between 'show' and 'tell' is to look at an example:

✓ **Tell:** Abigail was very cross. Her parents were so mean to her. She hated them for grounding her. She hated her dad most of all.
✓ **Show:** Abigail stamped her foot on the ground. "That's not fair. You can't do that to me, dad. You can't ground me!" Her dad arched an eyebrow. "You brought it on yourself, young lady," he said. "Maybe *now* you'll learn to do as you are asked."

Genre and Style

Genre offers a kind of 'toolkit' so that a writer knows what should be included, within a particular type of story. Each genre has a specific set of commonly agreed characteristics, including location, plot events, dialogue, vocabulary, characters, clothes, etc. For instance, a crime story would

70

probably include a detective, a criminal, a crime, a police station, a murder weapon, and so on. Get your students to choose a genre, and then to identify all the aspects they would expect to see within it. This is the 'expected pattern' for the reader, but it is not the only one; often writing is more stylish when the writer subverts the reader's expectations. To do this:

- ✓ Get your students to subvert genres in some way, for instance by incorporating elements of one genre (comedy) into another contrasting one (crime).
- ✓ Take a character from one genre and drop him/her/it into an entirely new setting. For example, putting the Big Bad Wolf into a chat show.
- ✓ Use a form from one genre, such the classic fairy story, to write a piece in another genre, for instance a Western.
- ✓ Subvert the classic stereotypes, as Babette Cole does in her book 'Prince Cinders', in which Cinders has to tidy up after his three hairy brothers.
- ✓ Create new genres, by blending elements of two familiar ones. For instance, what would happen if your students mixed Science Fiction with Scandinavian Noir?
- ✓ Experiment with turning a piece of fiction into a piece of non fiction. A genre story rewritten as a leaflet, a news report, an interview, and so on.

26716046R00044

Printed in Great Britain
by Amazon